This Journal Belongs To:

Name _____

Address _____

_____

Phone _____

Email _____

*We hope you enjoyed using this book. It would really help u
a lot if you would take a moment to leave a review. Thanks.*

---

*Snappy Journals
Check out our book catalog at:*

amazon.com/author/snappyjournals

Made in the USA
Las Vegas, NV
11 October 2021